Still Life

Poetry by

Elizabeth Evans Landrum

ISBN: 978-1-716-09803-1

Cover art by Elizabeth Reutlinger

The author gratefully acknowledges the poetry editors of the following journals where some of these poems first appeared: Shark Reef (*Why Write?*), Soundings Review (*Erosion*), Glass Mountain (*Afternoon Drift*), River lit (*Half-told Stories*), Grey Sparrow (*Late-night Wrestling ,Tension of Opposites*), Cirque (*Teachable Moment, Morning Fog*), Plainsongs (*Dining Out*), Raven Chronicles (*In a World of Danger*).

Other poems earlier appeared in two chapbooks (*How to Save the World* and *Refuge on the Rock*) by Lopez Island poets

Still Life

For my wife, Valerie Green, who makes all poetry possible…

CONTENTS

Part One: By Way of Words and Dreams

Part Two: Narrow Slices of Life

Part Three: Slim Slivers of Time

Part Four: Parting the Curtains

By Way of Words and Dreams

To know what you're going to draw,
you have to begin drawing.
What I capture in spite of myself interests me
more than my own ideas. — Pablo Picasso

What if we only wanted openings, the immortality of the unfinished, the uncut thread, the incomplete, the open door, and the open sea?
— Rebecca Solnit

Why Write?

Otherwise...
I twirl through mazes of cornstalks
without noticing
the flaxen beauty of the bounty,
the sweet musty scent
that mingles
muddy boots with damp husks,
and I'm blind to the raptor's view
of patterns of maize.

Otherwise...
through all the twirl
I miss
a dragonfly's flutter in my chest,
a tiny surge of thirst,
dewdrops nesting in petals.

Otherwise...
there are no commas,
no exclamation points,
and everything,
everything evaporates.

Not/Now

Not as soon as your calendar is blank
and your papers are all in rank and file
Not some time after others leave
and you're deeply steeped in the void
Not because rain is pooling in the garden
or whenever your harried brain has cooled
Not after the cumin has married coriander
and all the news is stale
Not someday
when your muse decides to hover
Not only under the cover of dawn
Not waiting to be altered
or disturbed
Not after all of your "But.."s have stalled

But
Now

Let the beckoning blank page
and the pen's smooth flow
settle and
propel you

There

Begin

I write to begin the day

(after Zubair Ahmed)

I used to think that
I could create time
I was wrong
time creates me
my rituals set a rhythm
that has no rhythm
my rituals begin
with a hand barely moving
warmed by a coffee mug
marks on a page
a hand moves but I don't notice
how the words fall together
black and not black
spaces to hold emotion
I create things
like my breakfast
of berries and yogurt
matter that doesn't matter
but words that do
loop and unloop
as destiny unfolds at my table
I will not surrender to clocks
I write to begin the day

O

Do you delight in being the opus
for every conceivable ode
following down the score —
an oboe duo, solo piano,
and oh, those ostinatos,
on through the bows,
the flowers, the encores,
and then, the last to go?

oh, O, do you blush
if your bow comes out
as bow or row as row
when you had no control?
Can you breathe if you're locked
in a box? Did you cringe
when some unbecoming circumflex
was placed on your head, only
to sound out another odd tone?

Once there was a simple door
to enter you — the primitive loop
we all made with crayons. Today
I scroll for fonts that draw you clean,
proud, perfectly round, although
in some larger cases, ovals will do.
But please, no curlicues, halos
or slants. If you sit a bit heavy
on those fine hips, or your sides
breathe slightly outward, don't worry,
it's just that you need to fit in,
no matter how strong your circle.

O, you need no one beside you
to support your importance, yet
when two of you stick together
something new will bloom —
the hoot of a loon, doves cooing,
once one lonesome cow
now soothed, now cocooned
in the cool of the moon.

O, when I say your name,
you are an open porthole,
a breath of air.
I never stop longing
for that honed down tone,
that moment to breathe
through rounded lips
with just a bit of throat,
to float on home
in a clear and lingering
O

Half-told Stories

Blithely I write
comfortable conclusions
for half-told stories,
make believe
I can size the space
between a hand that pushes
the pen and
its demise, pretending
something will last —
the poet
or the poem.

Then a presence or
absence never imagined
blasts in,
changes the chapter,
demanding another revision.
The chaste paper waits.
Again, I pick up the pen.

Unbound

She had horses who said they weren't afraid.
She had horses who lied.
(from "She Had Some Horses" by Joy Harjo)

Because I live with a fear
of being trapped

in small enclosures I dream
myself in a coffin

puffins circling in a teacup
a pigeon caught in a downspout

This morning I read a poem with these lines:
She had horses who were much too shy, and kept quiet
in stalls of their own making.

Now I am the paddock
and the horse at full gallop

I am the forest ablaze
the wind and the lines of control

I am tendrils of snowdrops pushing up
and the snow

and the coffin
with pillows of satin

Poetry 101: Controlled Chaos

It's like riding a horse, they told me
— reins too tight and she'll balk,
too loose and she'll take off,
like my flat-coat retriever after a deer, racing
through thickets of blackberry brambles
lost in a state of confusion.

But it was just that taste of strangeness
I craved, like lavender bitters for my bourbon,
so I mounted her bare back,
elbows piercing her withers, fingernails
poked in her crest, knees steeled to her flanks.
And she threw me.

Then, with clucking sounds and a hand full of oats,
I coaxed her into the paddock.
I rifled through tack room cabinets for halter,
blinders, tether, and whip, then
worked her for weeks, finally learning
why they call it breaking.

I offered up one red apple, palm open, hand steady
as a farrier's, and she read me, resisted a minute,
knowing full well I might expect something in return.
She extended her lips, her mouth frothed with
sloppy chomping, and she streaked away,
leaving me dazed and complaining
like a spider dropped in a sticky sink.

Longing to swim behind her generous eyes, blink
those extravagant lashes, cool drafts wafting
through my nostrils, I gave her the name Calliope,
though she did just fine without it.
And on my walls, I sketched her equine energy,
like ochre stains on Paleolithic caves.

Finally friends. Some days I called her beast.
Some days I asked her to shoulder my burdens.
She'd stiffen, lower her head obediently,
as if I could ever be her master.
Then I lashed a raft of branches onto her back,
and we sauntered, side by side, until
black sap oozed from cuts in the wood.
We agreed to abandon the deadweight.

Next, I suggested we try something lighter,
showed her dressage moves, the change of legs,
some lateral patterns. And when she danced,
in her chosen cadence, I followed.
Soon I could see she was itching to sprint,
so I entered her in some high-stakes races.
We almost lost everything then.

Today we move down meandering dreamtrails.
She chooses the turns. She sets the pace.
And I ride, just for the pleasure of riding.
Still, I am wanting
more trails, more meadows, more
damp sandy beaches, more long days
when Calliope rides me.

Signs

You know how it is
when you're listening to the evening news
and you've just overcooked the asparagus,
then you drop a bowl of pumpkin guts on the floor,
and all the love evaporates from your kitchen,
so you decide it's time to give it up, wait
for tomorrow, make a sandwich, go to bed.

But then, you remember that morning's dream —
you're trapped in an attic with your dead mother
when a troupe of improv actors, speaking in tongues,
picks you to kick around on the stage,
but their shoes are glued to the floor.

And you think about that same afternoon
when you were searching for your work boots
stashed in the attic, and discovered their soles
had decomposed — pieces of plastic
scattered like dried leaves and ash
across the wooden floor.
You called out for your mother

but you didn't know why.
So, you wonder
if it all means something
worthy of your attention, or
was it just
another crappy day?

Shortcuts

This morning asleep through two alarms,
I wander deep in another world.
Soft feet rustle, muffle the crush of leaves
scattered across the yard next-door.
The house is empty,
the owner dead.

I recognize this shortcut to forest trails,
morning light through the trees, my beacon.
Something beckons me to the entrance.
Nose pressed against massive glass doors,
I feast on alabaster nudes, blown glass spirals,
canvas landscapes displayed in the foyer.

Next, I track my path through the forest,
return through the same neighbor's yard,
slink past children in the backyard pool
laughing, splashing, shrieking *Marco Polo*!
Potted ferns embrace the water's edge,
a flash of fall leaves dotting the surface.

Another pass by the entry glass. I startle.
Over my shoulder stands a shivering figure
in her white terrycloth robe, collarbones exposed,
broken flip-flops. Silently, she follows my steps
to the property line. When I begin to tell her
I'm not a snoop — just starving for art —

she politely requests permission to cut
through my back yard
should she go calling on neighbors.
I ask if she's hungry too.
Our syncopated laughter is strangled
by the buzz of a third alarm.

And what of the dream?
And what of the poem?
Well, there are no shortcuts to meaning.
But this much I can say —
it was mine.
Now, it is yours.

Narrow Slices of Life

Human beings are works in progress that mistakenly think they're finished. The person you are right now is as transient, as fleeting and as temporary as all the people you have ever been. — Dan Gilbert

Disenchantment is the blessing of becoming yourself. — Rebecca Solnit

Each has to enter the nest
made by the other imperfect bird – Rumi

On a dull afternoon

Unfocused, unfinished,
not quite to bored,
I hear lapping at the shore,
grab my old cane pole,
step down an overgrown path
past thickets of twigs,
mossy boulders hiding behind,
like faces —
friends, I imagine,
but not always.

There is something
in the air I can't quite taste,
my tongue unwilling
to venture. Is it something
now arriving, or
just gone by?
I move on,
thinking it's only me,
foolish even to wonder,
but not always.

The beach is slick, uneven.
I could not guess how far
might be too far.
Staying safe, foothold sure,
where the rocks are dry and
the water's lap beyond reach,
I cast my line. Sometimes
we pull up demons, but not always.

I tell myself what counts
is the leaning in,
the gazing down
into pockets and pools,
their constant circling,
droplets dimpling the surface,
sure that sometimes
what seems like rain
is nothing more than that.

Dining out

(after Edward Hopper's *Room in New York* and *Chop Suey*)

So many people want to know
how they are this evening,
if they'd like to leave
their coats at the door, or drape them
over the backs of their chairs,
if they'd like lemon slices in their water,
how rare he prefers his filet, and
if tonight she'll take her salad dressed
or naked, vinaigrette on the side.

But what she wants to know is how many
more times they'll be sitting here
or there, their wine glasses filled again
and again with empty conversations,
pretending to care about each other
more than the tang of the hollandaise,
the night's surly server, or words overheard
from the neighboring table.

Today, after she checked their calendar
for conflicts, she watched herself place
the red beret above one eyebrow
as he looped his best striped tie
like always, polished his shoes
with a lick of his fingers, cracked each
knuckle twice. She could smell the smolder
from the night before.

They did not speak
until the air was so frozen and thick
it had to be broken. This time he held
the ice pick. He asked which restaurant
she'd chosen. *The same as last time,*
she said, because she did not want
to consider an alternative.

Erosion

Do you remember
the times I went away
just for the pleasure
of returning
Did you say
it was too long
too far
too often

Can you recall which
direction we faced
as our web wove itself
into masses too dense
to untangle
and our plans spilled
over the bedroom floor

pages and pages
of unspoken words
dreams fallen
like a chain
corroded from its buoy
reeling in the tide

Was it then
three years ago or four
your porch or mine
you said you wanted
something more
and we stood silent
dew dripping
from the eaves
waiting
for the next move

Fledgling in Distress

I awaken to a dream of you —
back turned, shirttail flapping.
Did you fall out of love with me
before you knew it? Or just
before I did? In love, love,
out of love — maybe somewhere
there's a language for it.

I watch from my bedroom window
as a yellow fledgling quivers,
clinging to the edge of its nest,
everything invested in
a thin weave of thistledown,
bark, and spider silk
fastened to a delicate sapling.

There was a time it nestled
in the protection of parents,
secure for a while, seeds
delivered beak to beak,
safe from invaders, warm
through the storms.

There comes a time to try
those untested wings, no matter
how loud the squawk, how high
the nest, how hard the ground.
A tiny goldfinch atilt in the wind,
waiting for courage
to test her lift.

Broken in the Rut

We wade into the damp dawn
finding signs of black-tailed deer
that nightly wander these island acres
between grassy bed and browse.

Cracked boughs, stripped saplings
hungover from drinking testosterone
and tension released
in the evening's flogging.

You who has lived in the city
think it something special,
this peak of the rut when ruddy bucks
stake their claim, leaving signals

for some unsuspecting doe,
while they toughen and bulk their necks
for tomorrow's antler battles.
What you call rousing, I call broken.

I scour for what can be scavenged
from this scourge of indifferent brutality.
Skin-shredded saplings, cambium
exposed, slick-raw and weeping.

What chance do they have —
wounds so deep and young
and no way to feed? Broken,
like one shimmering wing
of a grounded damselfly.

I find pine branches dismembered,
dangling, held by a slip. So I snip
twig from branch, branch from trunk,
until the damage can't be seen.
Broken,
like promises we once made,
leaving room for forgiveness.

Regret
wears like a heavy overcoat
its yawning pockets laden with rocks —

What she spent on that one pair of shoes
Others she didn't buy
because they seemed too flashy
Rooms she was too shy to enter
Rooms that consumed her
All the sashimi she never tasted
And a few she did
The trip to Antarctica she didn't take
while it was still possible
Memories of Mexico dropped in the well
A menu of things she inhaled
And some she didn't, like the whiff of
cerulean sweet-peas before they browned
Letters from her mother tossed in the waste
The alarm clock she left in pieces
never learning how it worked
That day she went rushing past a young
barred owl standing stunned on the road
certain that someone else would help
Words that flew
like sparks in any hasty conflagration
Words not spoken
before the final goodbye…

She'll shuffle under the weighty cloak
loading more stones as she goes
until her shoulders crumple
her knees buckle and
she cannot climb
or
might she decide
to simply
slip it
off?

Late -night Wrestling

Every stray cat that yowls
from a distant porch
sounds the same
when you're trying to sleep.

Restless ghosts begin their chants,
signal wolves to your doorstep, calling
for winds that howl in from the north.
They grab at your bedsheets

as you strive to empty
your tangled mind,
to lift a heavy heart
from the well of its losses.

You must carry it carefully,
start from the bottom,
climb each rung
until the light appears

then ask for a hand.
It will be there —
the calm when all the ghosts
and cats are voiceless again,

the wolves have drifted on.
Only then can you hear the beat
of your own breathing ---
like a talking-drum repeating

Come Back Home

Arriving

I told them
I would not make this island Home —
too small, too still, too spare
for one who must be doing.

Yet to her I came to cleanse myself
of all the leavings, breathe peace,
savor a taste of something new.
She cradled my head in the gentlest hand,
bathed my feet in a different balm, soothed
my unhealed heart beside an un-still sea
and made me
stop.

She taught me how
dawn drapes the landscape
in pallets of pastels,
pries open the senses with
mist on a cheek, salt on a tongue,
patterns of wind in a wave
before the mind
can find its daily patter.

She ushered me home
where my breathing catches
on an eagle's wing
and I am content to stare
for hours amused by rhythms
of whitecaps
that dance on the flow,
then dive, then return.

Today I am studying
how dusk dulls
the day's keen edge,
blurs the seam
between the steel gray sea
and a slightly lighter sky,
pencils in sketches,
then erases its shadings.
No, this is not small, not spare.
Never   still.

One Egg or Two

First, not even my breakfast egg could stay.
Like anything easily shattered by a clumsy hand
it rolled so slowly
it seemed motionless as it
toppled off the edge
twisting down
down
to the slick tiled floor
splattered like dead words lost
in any tiny distraction
yellow glue
s t r e t c h i n g
into the next room
before I could stop it.
Then, it was the smell of it that
lingered
on my dishtowel
and fingernails
long after
the clean-up.

I could hardly stand to try again
until you offered
your cupped palm to
cradle it from the carton
walk it across
that same hard floor
to the skillet
where I could break it
into the melting butter
and remember how
I like it fried
with a still-soft center.

Morning Fog

Streaks of pink shoot through blue
to sing the morning in.
In silence, we watch from the window
of our loft, feet entwined, soft
in cotton and down. The fog yawns low,
blankets the straits, curls up
against the island's prow.
You ask if I see it too.

It is here that I am lost and found
the trusted tones of your breathing
and mine entrained
by chance and practice.
It is here we are birthed
under the cover of dreams,
each day new.

And when time's demands must
draw us down,
we'll leave a trail of crumbs
to return us to this space
above the constant din, where we
re-discover ourselves, emerging
blind, in love with
the unequalled eloquence
of the unseen.

Teachable Moment

From my own small town history
I knew where they had been,
and where they had not.
It's cities like this, cafes like this
that seem foreign to them ---
unpronounceable items
on the menu, and women like us
in our tattered jeans and
tailored shirts.

All evening during dinner,
my hand resting on your thigh,
I didn't notice them watching,
didn't see the whispering until
it was loud enough to hear
Did you see them? Do you think...?
And in that instant, I knew we were
a teachable moment, the ones
who didn't look like they expected,
an image they would keep.

You moved my hand so gently
I hardly sensed it, but still
I could give you a certain look
and familiar smile
that said everything,
and not just to us.

at the Hearts and Love Bakery

It was a good enough request at first —
that wedding cake she said she wanted.
He was sure he heard it right.
Pink and green roses on top with
those anonymous plastic figures —
two wives, two tiaras, one heart framing.
Five tiers — alternating chocolate and vanilla,
all iced with white, curtained in chocolate curls
that will surely conspire to wilt or break
if the temperature is off.

He enters the bakery at 3 am, skyline dark,
a few dim lights fringing the streets.
Lately, his confidence shattered
like a shot glass on concrete, he needs this
to be a masterpiece. He shucks his
black leather jacket and red baseball cap,
dons the white apron, toque, and
floured hands of his daily routine,
shuffles across the old oak floorboards
ignoring the usual self-insults
that could easily suffocate a cake.
He pulls five sized pans from the shelf,
breathes in, rehearsing his plan
to add more hearts
on the top of each layer.

Winter Solstice

Remind me
how the light appears
later
into dawn, then stretches
beyond our five o'clock tea,
soon to widen our course.

But now?
It is glinting on distant peaks,
singing.
I needn't send for spring.
Not yet.
Our house is put in order,
sealed tight against the coming cold,
its warm breath just enough
to make a candle flicker.

Is this Monday or
Tuesday? No matter.
Lentil soup is at a simmer now.
Your platter of warm rye bread rests
yawning under a damask cloth,
scents of yeast and lemon
summoning

this moment, rare
as certitude, common
as prayer,
opening slowly,
closing fast.

Have I missed another
in anticipation of the next?
The cost of a blink
too dear to bear,
please remind me
of the light.

Summer Solstice

I can't recall the chill
of damp dark December,
though I dread its return.
Yet here by the campfire
in our rickety wooden chairs,
two dogs asleep at our feet, it seems
as far away as the stars we applaud
when they peek from behind
their shredded vapor curtains
brushed against the twilight sky.
Now I remember the beauty
that lives only in shadows.

Firelight captures our focus as
we talk of summer's insistence,
winter's acceptance, on this
two-season island, while
everything else disappears
degree by degree, into the
not-quite-dark of midnight.
Strange how stars and sparks,
burning wood and a stone circle
seem to dissolve our disguises,
leaving us here searching
for an opening
in the core of dancing embers.

<u>How Terribly Strange</u>

Time, time time, see what's become of me
— Simon and Garfunkel

Where is there air for clarity
when smoke surrounds, and years
keep disappearing behind me, hours
gliding over my shoulders, soundless
as an owl in flight?

It's not yet night,
but it's been quite a long time
since morning. I can hardly remember
breakfast, nursery rhymes or the voices
of those who once recited them.

My chapters are titled by houses
and partners — stories linked
in overlapping versions of myself,
barely recognizable now
as I come into understanding.

My reflection reveals but one
familiar face, now seventy, now
saddled with Mother's jowls,
eyes burnished with contentment
still looking out for possibilities,

lips parted in slow exhalations —
not a word, but a whistle
enticing me to savor what I've become
and welcome this feast of evenings,
each salty, sweet and bitter bite.

Slim Slivers of Time

The truth is, we know so little about life, we don't really know what the good news and what the bad news is.
—- Kurt Vonnegut

We know not yet what we have done, still less what we are doing
— Henry David Thoreau

Life can only be understood backwards; but it must be lived forwards —Soren Kierkegaard

In a dream

I see myself walking across a suspension bridge,
bare toes probing for the loose moving rungs
barely lashed together by unraveling rope,
my hands groping in the darkness
for something fixed to hold.

I can hear the turbulence below,
the churn and bash of waves
against a ragged shore,
while I act unafraid
and pretend there
will be bulkheads
strong enough
to stay the
rising
tides.

the tree which moves some to tears of joy is in the eyes of others only a green thing which stands in the way — William Blake

i. Yew

Sprouted by a stroke of luck
in this unlikely lottery,
she took her stand, welcoming
her slow-growing reach.
In gold shafts and blue shadows
of an understory she remained
patient, frugal, never lamenting
her lowly fifty-foot stature or
homely appearance, yearning
for nothing but sun, rain, fungus,
the recurrent workings of Earth.

She endured time's lacerations
as weevils gnawed her needles,
deer feasted and cankers formed,
as winds ripped her branches,
jettisoned limbs from above, as her
darkened pages of bark peeled away,
exposing her red tender skin.

She covered her wounds and
branched anew,
thrust tangles of roots deep
into the drying earth,
stashed food for her future,
pumping water by gallons
through xylem to crown.
Run and flow,
rupture and repair —
the recurrent workings of life.

ii. You

Blind you came.
Blinded by a plot line
of profit called progress.
Blind to her history,
her push for survival
through ten of your lifetimes,
you scanned the landscape,
squinting into the distance.

She was simply in the way.
You wore on your forearm
a tattoo of the Earth, the word
"Mother" inscribed across it,
and in your grip a chainsaw,
weighted with anticipation.
How facile the kill when
"It's just what we do".

No prayer of apology.
No chant for gratitude.
Why bother? You
were the only one there.
But you heard the crack,
the crash,
the stunned silence after.

Gaslighting America

a mind can be undone
when slow drips
of doubt
hypnotize
by relentless ticks
like a metronome
until
we are staring
into a dazzling sky
where stars
have lost
their power
to amaze us
and sanity slips
soundless
as burning wings

Letter From Space

Dear humans,

So far, we cannot explain
why multitudes deny the truth,
or argue over language

while others insist the earth is dying
and they can't yet guess
your planet's age. You're sure that

nature is constantly changing,
and species come and go.
But yours will too

while you pretend it is you
who could stay
to repair the damage.

More omens drone on
while we watch you rumble up
to that last bus stop

where rain burns
your eyelashes and the sun
drenches your sleeves. Lost

without street signs you stand
swooned by a kestrel as she
laces the stained glass sky

while her lingering cry
seems to elude you
like the warnings

written all over your oceans
— too deep to hear,
no matter how loud.

Talking with children about climate change

i.

Walking this tightrope barefoot
you cling to the balance pole
as it shifts in the wind, tips
toward an urgent push to action
then dips
into the abyss of impotence

ii.

You know how it is
to hear the children crying
for the lonely lean polar bear
in their bedtime stories, or
their visions of fish floating
in oceans overtaking their town.
If you're there to stroke their shoulders,
do you say it will all be OK,
swallow that stone in your throat?
Do you dare to admit
it's not so remote?

iii.

When they conjure up a Superpower
that is sure to stop the warming,
do you join in? Or
crush that dream
under the anvil of truth?
How hard will it be to confess
what you can't foresee
when they ask
where it will be safe to live
when they're grownups, or
if there will be butterflies then?

iv.

When they want to know *Why?*
what words will you choose
to explain
how We
did This
to Them?

In a World of Danger

Some begin each day offering orchids,
mangoes, rice and papaya to gods
who might visit their spirit house
then drape the prow of a long-tailed boat
with colorful sashes and garlands of lotus.
Some chant prayers for the sharpened arrow,
for the cougar, a moonlit path home,
while others knit, count stitches,
repeat a poem before sleep.

Once I shared a table with other women
discussing what they carry each time
they walk through a city's dark parking lot.
A nurse holds her clamps and scalpel
close in her pocket. Another showed us
her hot-pink "lipstick" pepper-spray case.
When asked what I take, I said: *My wife* —
her eyes and ears sharpened by experience,
mine dulled by denial.

But what of the mothers,
the fathers, trying to breathe
before the school bell rings?
Some will brush their daughters' hair
counting an even number of strokes, or
kiss a son's forehead exactly three times,
then walk them up to the entrance repeating
you'll be fine   you'll be fine   you'll be fine

For the Sake of Water
(after Dorianne Laux)

No matter where the water, its clarity,
source or scarcity, we all must partake of it.
We rise and give thanks to the water carriers—
the girls who walk
through orange-hot sand
steadying 40-pound cans on their heads,
helicopters hovering over wildfires, canteens
for the trenches, teams of samaritans
dropping jugs across the Sonoran desert,
and my underground PVC.

Bless water.
Somehow it always finds me,
determined to keep me from looking
beyond my close horizon —
this substance that calls to everyone,
this noun without synonym or opposite,
definitions sodden with significance.

This morning, as I awaken, my lips
abrasive as sandpaper, tongue glued
to the roof of my mouth, I reach
for the glass primed at my bedside.
What do I know of thirst?
There, in my dream —
a thousand parched mouths entreating
as they veer between torpor and hope —
everyday citizens of Sanaa, Chennai,
Tripoli, Pavillion and Flint, waiting
like drained roots straining
under their charred forest carpets,
waiting
like a ship grounded in a receding tide,
waiting for salvation.
I offer them blossoms and teardrops.

All day it continues — our parched earth
breaking apart in pieces, each dry riverbed
reaching toward another, strangers
everywhere stretching, sharing sips
from a tin cup as I pass by, dreaming
of the next hallowed shower
to drench my dusty pores.

Swimming in the Wreckage

I used to think my spider plants
would persist in dropping babies
from their macrame hangers,
and my Christmas cactus
would push its pink trumpets
November after November,
if I managed the light just right.
I hoped that dope would at least
elongate the weekends
while men fired rockets at the moon
and the Vietcong.

Once, I believed the testaments
of reporters and preachers,
the Declaration of Independence,
and lovers who promised to be faithful.
Now one fourth of my high school class
and some of those lovers are dead.
Everywhere there is fallout
from the rocket's red glare, and
nowhere to hide.

I wish I could say I still believe
in the Thanksgiving storybook and
other fictions like inalienable rights
endowed by some ethereal creator,
proof that our flag is there. Still,
the pursuit of happiness remains
mine to choose, so I'll stay
close to the voices of poets,
repeat stories that sustain me and
words that satisfy, like J u s t i c e,
if only because I like the sound.
There are life rafts bobbing
in the flotsam. I will not drown.

A Time It Was

While the battles outside were raging
and a hard rain continued to fall,
pictures of caskets and jungle jackets
were served up with supper each night.
It was a time when we knew our neighbors
tuned in to the same three sources
and we all believed Cronkite —
his face, his words, and once his tears,
unmasked by bitter truths.

What I miss is a time when movements
were made of music, and all those lyrics
roosted in our hearts.
Hands and voices raised in the psychedelic air,
woven, like chords, for a cause.
Gauzy skirts, bellbottoms, bare feet in the dirt,
blankets over our shoulders.
Blankets tossed across city parks
and campus lawns.
How open we were to each other
when one acoustic guitar
would multiply by scores
and a few electrics in special hands
drew multitudes, shoulder to shoulder,
swaying, chanting, turned on
by any chimes of freedom.

Imagine all the people
— half a million at once,
singing for our lives, pleading
to give peace a chance.
How could we not believe
we could overcome?

They say everything can be replaced,
that every distance is not near.
I can hardly see the face
of anyone who joined me there.
Today we are nomads wandering
through drier lands, tangled up in
blue connections we bought
with all technology gave us,
thirsting for what
it has taken away.

Yet when darkness drops in
I can listen to our music
to see my reflection,
hug tight to my chest
that feeling when
any day now
I might see my light
come shining
from the west
unto the east.

A half-blind raccoon in my basement
once glared at me from the corner
of her one good eye, then turned
face-on to her menace.
Nose high, lip curled, both eyes
in a squint, she growled, hissed,
spit her last-ditch statements
while I stood my ground, tall
and wide-eyed terrified.

Today, as I consume one more
Senate hearing with breakfast,
I study the visage of fear,
watch how we open, then
close ourselves to the specter
of shame. I listen for the tremors
of voice that enter
when we speak bare truths
into the faces of critics.

Half-blind. Red-faced. We
all demean some Other we fear,
hands cupping our ears.
How like that raccoon,
we wrinkle our noses and squint,
spit, snarl, and bare our teeth
when cornered or
find ourselves reeling
on the verge of losing
everything we thought
we could keep.

Dining In (April, 2020)

Everyone wants to know
when they can go back.
Back to dining out, back to work
in an office, back to school, go
back to the stage and stadium, to
churches, temples, parties. Return
to something they call "normal" —
back to the games they know, like
Monopoly where the luck of the draw
lets the winner take all, or
Musical Chairs when stealth
and speed mean having a seat
while the others steadily leave.

What I want to know is
how do we go forward,
leaning in to something
we haven't learned to play —
games of imagination,
like shadow puppets on the wall
where spaces between us
mean coming together,
building new places
where people can trust

that when they fall backwards
there will be arms to catch them,
and tongues can taste of shared values
like the sweetness of bread,
where the unnoticed become
noticed, and every day is seasoned
with pirouettes around living rooms,
leaps down empty streets, operas
belted from balconies,
birds that fly in a clear open sky.

Something is happening while nothing is happening

In pockets of stillness
the blossom withholds its unfurling
until the time is right.
In the middle of a pandemic, we learn
to stay at home, to live alongside our
uninvited guest that keeps nibbling
like beetles
at the delicate edges of our illusions.

We've been jolted into seeing
that something unseen
can take our breath,
change our cells, charge ahead
toward some unknowable goal
while we wait, lost,
some days willing
to go deeper into the fog-filled woods
in search of something we can't name.

And here we are
no less astonished than that day
we witnessed the sun's eclipse
and birds went out of kilter
and the light was all wrong.
Though the coming was predicted,
we could feel the ancient terror
of the sun's disappearance,
relief when the colors returned,
surprise when they seemed more vivid
than just the day before.

Yes, we bounced back then,
hurried home to a world
both diminished and expanded,
having been all at once infected
by the same strange favor. Yet,
even transcendence is transient
as the absence of light.
How do we now dance with
this contagious disquiet,
fly for a while out of kilter,
keeping a window open
into the dark?

Penance

As the bright light falters,
and shadows surround
the graveyards we've created,
remind us
how lizards once slipped
from a burnt land
only later to fly,
how bats will emerge
from narrow cracks
wherever darkness hints,
and ants will build
more super-colonies
by sharing their labor.

Ease our contrition
with stories of the Phoenix,
of seeds and saplings
still sealed underground.
Teach us
when the remnants
of human folly evaporate
like fog left by breath,
how Earth will re-edit herself,
every facet and blemish polished
like a diamond
containing the memory
of a future.

Parting the Curtains

Everything ends in mystery…we have to think about the unthinkable, which is what religion does and science does too.
—Ray Bradbury

Imagination is the only weapon in the war against reality. —Lewis Carroll

The immensity beyond our withering comprehension is more than humbling; it is humiliating that we should take ourselves so seriously. — Stanley Plumy

Tutorial

If you have watched the colors slowly shuffle
along the shore of a neighboring island,
gold to brick to sable, if
you have seen how each gray and silver ripple
streaks the sea in synchrony
with cloud, with wind and current, then
you might understand why
there cannot be another dawn
just like this,
and why we try to capture the light,
though we know it will dwindle
like fireflies in a jar.

If you can be focused,
poised as the heron, observing
as each thought evaporates,
each sensation fades
into the next frame, and if
you can remain long enough
to lose yourself
in time's illusions, then
you might know memory
as a chameleon
and tomorrow as air.

If you've been taken to your knees
by the beast you hadn't noticed
charging behind you, if
you've been rapt in your distractions
so you missed the sleight of hand
that pulled the rabbit from your hat, then
you might be asking how to flex
for the next unseen clip,
or maybe it's time to set your pace
to the rhythm of your heart
and learn to be enchanted
by surprise.

Twisted Truths

Life's school has taught us
five is often the sum of
two plus two, the world is not
flat, not round, not even a speck
undetected from outer spaces,
and vast worlds exist
in underground places
only a stone's throw away.

Yet we make our plans as if
we could see it all clearly, as if
we were safe at home, looking out
from our glass houses.
Forever judging our books
by the back of their jackets, afraid
to go the way of the curious cat,
we perceive every peg and hole
to be round, and hope
to be able to manage a mallet.

Why should we hang our cradles
on boughs that will break
and not on the contrails of dreams
while we still can be enchanted
by our moon's dark side?

Although we will listen
for the clap of one hand,
for the tree that falls in the forest,
we'll tear through the bush
in search of that one little bird
we'd like to hold onto
or a lily to gild,
foregoing the rosebud
too quickly shriveled.

Easy to forget we are the eyes
of the beholder, mouths speaking
words too often too loud
for our actions, heads turning
toward the bliss of ignorance.
Hard to remember the riches
that are found, not growing on trees,
but buried where we've sown them
deeper than our skin, still ripe
for the reaping.

Ode to Edges

Oh you who love clear edges/ more than anything…
watch the edges that blur. —Adrian Rich

It's the edge of night I love
when all colors drain
from the land. It's the edge
of a body where skin meets air
or the softness of fingertips.

Property lines with no signs —
boundaries told only by history
or nature. And the edge of a wing
that cuts through air, tilting a bit
for balance and lift.

It's a shift in an argument
when some fixed idea adjusts,
widens to a new point of view.
I love the shapes of sunlight and
shadow made by a shade tree

or cloud. A split in earth's crust
that offers a glimpse
into the yawning abyss.
It's the richness of liminal time —
that gray in-between

when the ticking stops
and all you can hear
is your heartbeat.
Even the present moment
is an edge,

each evanescent sliver of time
teetering on the brink
of a promise.
It's the corner of an eye,
the dawning light,

the places where
endings and beginnings live
together, dropping jewels
from the holes
in their pockets.

Tension of Opposites

Don't ask me to explain
why clarity unlocks by confusion,
why expecting nothing satisfies,
how time will quicken the dead
or change to stay.

We live with obvious ghosts
crowding our hallways,
benign poisons in the pantry,
silent screams floating up
from a basement full of nothing.

Hold the taut line loose
where you might find me
lost, replete with emptiness.
For sometimes I crave hunger
and I may speak an honest lie.

Together we celebrate solitude,
remember what we did not forget.
Too often we're careless with the crystal,
but wholeness is made by the breaking.
Soon, patient impatience will soothe.

There's a pointless significance
to this lasting impermanence.
Come, welcome doubt,
for something old is in the making,
and you never know how far
you might travel
tethered to a wisp.

What if someone was listening
when you served rumors with the soup,
whispered *Share some with me, but don't tell*?
Listening, when you take cheap shots
at your brother, playing to his weaker side?

What if someone could listen to
the noises in your head
when you're reaching for sleep,
those cruel conversations that amble on
about your latest failings

and seemingly fatal flaws?
Or the prattle that plays
on the evening commute, those stories
where you star as the victim?
Someone could be listening

while you're talking over coffee
and you twist the simplest strands
into a knot you hope will hold, or
you're caught painting over the canvas
to hide the mess underneath.

And when you think you're alone
at dusk in the rain, breaking
through brush, angry roots
grabbing the toes of your boots,
thorns ripping your eyebrows,

so you pray out loud —
What if someone was listening?

How it happens

Not yet winter. Across the yard
shrubs begin to shiver,
cloaking themselves
in ice, gray clouds slung
over all that was recently green.
Hail drops tiny beads
so slow I can hear each
plink on a deck board,
unsure at first
if I truly detect the peppering.
More pellets pop, ping,
bounce across tabletops, ricochet
off rims of flowerpots as the chorus builds,
swelling to a crescendo of pelting
before trailing off toward
the inevitable departure.

I'm reminded of the popping
of kernels in our Jiffy-pop pan, the magic
expanding on the stovetop, how we listened
for that moment when we could slice
the bright aluminum packet and *make*
watching t.v. as much fun as
going to the movies. I'm thinking of
Friday nights with my older brother —
Twilight Zone or Parcheesi, the mixing bowl
on the coffee table brimming with popcorn,
our greasy fingers competing.
How does it happen? A synapse twists,
then a yellowing memory brightens.
Time dissolves the edges
like rain on salt.

There's a battering of ice on my roof,
a tapping I mistake for the prayer beads
on my doorknob that clack against glass
when I close out the world. Outside
every surface is stippled
with white. I watch pellets disappear
into puddles that form
in the pockets of my driveway,
how they turn softer
in motion, then, again frozen.

Exfoliation

Not like a garter snake discarding
his soiled patterned jacket of
diamonds and stripes,
multiple times a year,
unzipping his skin to
pull himself through,
inch by inch, in one
slow slithering wriggle,
scales unfolding from lip
and chin to tail, scraping through
rough rock tunnels to strip away
the dulled confinement, then
stretching, he flexes free, to
inhabit his slick fresh coat.

Not like the thin slivers of bark
that surround the Pacific yew —
gray scales peeling away in stages
measured by decades, like pages
weathered and torn, exposing
the red beneath to breathe
green air. Not like this
pas de deux—the curl,
the twist and push,
the unwitnessed
drop.
Now habitat,
now humus,
now life.

No, ours is a continuous invisible shift.
Forty thousand cells a day
slough to dust we inhale
or simply sweep away. Each month, each cell
replaced — palms, cheeks, shoulders,
fingertips reborn for the stroking.
Transformations while we sleep and
silent exchanges made in the quickstep dance
we all do together — you in your given skin,
me in my white protective shell.

Afternoon Drift

Come with me for a quiet kayak afternoon.
Let's share tales of our childhoods,
let our blades break the placid straits
then glide
past purple sea stars and urchins
clasped tight to the rocks
while a kingfisher rattles his disturbance
and gulls join a discordant chorus
in their herring-ball congregations.

Now let's turn back,
drift a while and listen.
These shores remember the smoke,
the cedar, the salmon, the welcoming poles.
The midden remembers the mollusks,
and the mollusk remembers its gills.
Those stumps remember the ten-foot
two-man saw. These lichen remember
the breezes of eons, and that black
pocked rock remembers the molten center.

Let's train our ears to symphonies
of the deep and her creatures,
listen for tales from our ocean home.
She remembers her ice ghosts
and bones — whales, nets, gunwales,
sailors — subsumed in silt and salt.
Let's skim the surface together.
Our tiny boat,
our sliver of time.

The Real Poem

Maybe the world, without us, is the real poem.— Mary Oliver

Yesterday I read about languages,
how they shape all knowledge,

how human minds expand
with each new one learned.

We take refuge in the simplicity
of naming,

in the precision of description,
as if we were not birds trying to fly

against the cages of words—
words fluid as our definitions,

words in and out of fashion,
music tuned to our ears.

Today I read about languages
of trees, roots, fungus, and food,

tangles of party-line conversations,
ancient information highways —

no borders, no claims, no disputes.
Cultures that bend for one another

blending in symbiotic symphonies played
under our feet, where what we call rotten

is sweet, and mosses we stomp across
matter to unseen matter.

Intelligence codes still unbroken.
Not to be silenced, we try.

We rattle around in our sterile cages,
pipettes, microbes, slides in hand

while the rest goes on without us. Listen.
Mother trees are suckling their young.

For now, let me settle my shoulder on soil,
speechless, bewildered,

cheek cushioned on moss,
rain in my face.

You are here because

you must know
something of love,

and your work,
whether or not it can be seen,
is not finished.

You drift, a speck
in the ocean's belly,
where every sound

conspires to distract
so you cannot sense
the water's fire.

There will be moments
when you may feel
the pull and the push,

and everything dances
as if nothing leads. Yes,
there will be sightings

of the Source,
though you will doubt
what your eyes remember.

You are here because
you know something
of love.   Pass it on.

ABOUT THE AUTHOR

Elizabeth Evans Landrum grew up in Louisville, Kentucky. After earning a Ph.D. in clinical psychology, she spent most of her 30 year career as a therapist in private practice, half in Louisville, and half in Edmonds, Washington. With her retirement came the opportunity to move full-time to her beloved island in the Salish Sea.

Her appreciation for poetry began as an adolescent but she became interested in writing poetry in her 50's. She now enjoys a quiet life on Lopez Island, relishing the beauty of her surroundings and time to create. Her poems have appeared in numerous print and on-line publications and in two chapbooks with other local poets. *Shelf Life*, her first poetry collection, was published in 2019.

www.ingramcontent.com/pod-product-compliance
Ingram Content Group UK Ltd.
Pitfield, Milton Keynes, MK11 3LW, UK
UKHW041644190726
13854UKWH00006B/2682

9 781716 098031